This Therapy Sessions Journal belongs to:

● ● ● ● ● ● ● ● ● ● ● ● ● ●

Therapy Sessions Journal

3rd Edition - June 2022

@adaytoremember_journals
adaytoremember.journals@gmail.com

INDEX

4 IMPORTANT INFORMATION
5 CRISIS RESOURCES CONTACT
6 INTRODUCTION
7 OUR THANK YOU NOTE TO YOU
8-9 HOW TO USE THIS JOURNAL
10-12 THERAPY SESSIONS SCHEDULE
13 THERAPY GOALS
14 THERAPY TOOLS I LEARNED

MONTH 1

16-25 THERAPY SESSION NOTES & SUGGESTIONS
26 CHECK UP PAGES
27 MEANINGFUL QUOTES & THOUGHTS

MONTH 2

28-37 THERAPY SESSION NOTES & SUGGESTIONS
38 CHECK UP PAGES
39 MEANINGFUL QUOTES & THOUGHTS

MONTH 3

40-49 THERAPY SESSION NOTES & SUGGESTIONS
50 CHECK UP PAGES
51 MEANINGFUL QUOTES & THOUGHTS

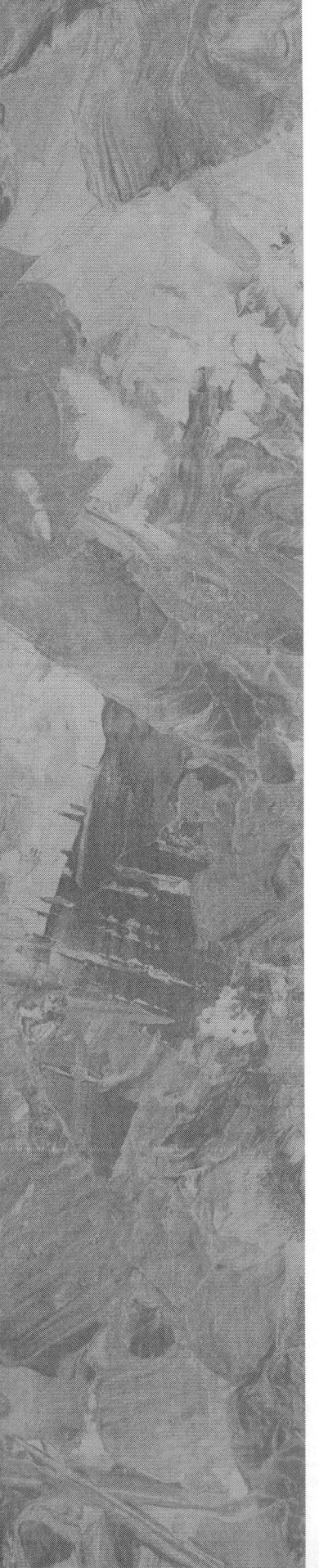

MONTH 4
52-61 THERAPY SESSION NOTES & SUGGESTIONS
62 CHECK UP PAGES
63 MEANINGFUL QUOTES & THOUGHTS

MONTH 5
64-73 THERAPY SESSION NOTES & SUGGESTIONS
74 CHECK UP PAGES
75 MEANINGFUL QUOTES & THOUGHTS

MONTH 6
76-85 THERAPY SESSION NOTES & SUGGESTIONS
86 CHECK UP PAGES
87 MEANINGFUL QUOTES & THOUGHTS

88-97 ADDITIONAL NOTES PAGES
98-100 GET TO KNOW OUR JOURNALS & JOIN OUR LAUNCH TEAM!

Important Information

PATIENT INFORMATION:

Name: _____

Phone: _____

E-mail: _____

THERAPIST #1 INFORMATION:

Name: _____

Phone: _____

E-mail: _____

THERAPIST #2 INFORMATION:

Name: _____

Phone: _____

E-mail: _____

THERAPIST #3 INFORMATION:

Name: _____

Phone: _____

E-mail: _____

Crisis Resources Contacts

US CRISIS RESOURCES:

US Suicide Prevention Lifeline: Call 1-800-273-8255
(The National Suicide Prevention Lifeline is a national network of local crisis centers that provides free and confidential emotional support to people in suicidal crisis or emotional distress 24 hours a day, 7 days a week).

Crisis Text Line: Text MHA to 741741
(You'll be connected to a trained Crisis Counselor. Crisis Text Line provides free, text-based support 24/7).

Youthline: Text teen2teen to 839863 or Call (877)968-8491
(A free 24-hour crisis, support, and helpline for youth. Talk to a teen volunteer daily from 4pm-10pm PST (and by adults at all other times!)).

Hotline for LGBTQ Youth (The Trevor project): Call 1-866-488-7386 or text START to 678678.
(A national 24-hour, toll free confidential suicide hotline for LGBTQ youth).

LOCAL HELP CENTERS:
Write below where you can find help in your neighborhood or country, if you're outside of the USA

Name:

Phone   Hours:

Description (eg. Teen support):

Name:

Phone   Hours:

Description (eg. Teen support):

Name:

Phone   Hours:

Description (eg. Teen support):

Name:

Phone   Hours:

Description (eg. Teen support):

Introduction

Therapy can be an act of love with ourselves. Sometimes we are going through situations that we cannot get out of alone, and we need the help of a professional therapist to open the doors to a new path, the self-knowledge path. Knowing ourselves does not prevent us from experiencing difficult situations, but it teaches us how to deal with them in the best way for our growth and healing.

This journal was designed to help all of us who seek self-knowledge as a way to reach a fuller and happier life. It has questions that will help us to reflect during and between therapy sessions, and that will help us do so in a positive way. In addition, it also includes a periodic reflection for each month, so that we can put ourselves in the place where we were and where we are now, and hopefully celebrate our progress in this wonderful process - the therapy journey.

With this journal you will be able to document highlights of your sessions, and will have a timeline of your transformation recorded in an organized and efficient way.

We hope that your healing will happen faster, and in a more intentional way with the help of this journal.

We trust that, with the help of therapy and your commitment to healing, your self confidence will grow and you will find true happiness again.

Good Luck!

Hello! We are Carla and Mila, two best friends, moms and passionate about journaling and mental health. We have attended therapy for years and we know the benefits that it can bring to our lives. We also know that write and reflect on the sessions can bring us organization and encouragement.

This journal was created from a patient point of view and it is meant to be a simple, practical and a useful tool for therapy patients.

We want to encourage you to keep writing and filling the pages with your sessions notes and progress that you will make over time.

Before you get started we'd like to introduce ourselves and THANK YOU for buying this journal!

We are 2 friends just starting a journey of entrepreneurship.
(We're now "grown ups," moms; Carla is based in the USA, and Milena in Brazil).

We are challenging ourselves to create 52 journals this year, ~1 per week!
We are so grateful for your support so far, and we invite you to follow our journey.

Our promise: to make EVERY customer happy

We hope this journal will help you discover the benefits of therapy by making it an easier and more organized process. We really believe that it will help bring improvements to your life and even to those around you.

But if for any reason you are not satisfied with your journal, please contact us directly; we will do our best to make you happy!

Your REVIEW means a lot to us!

And especially if you like this journal, would you please give us a couple minutes of your time and write a review on Amazon?

As we write this, this journal is brand new and has no ratings or reviews on Amazon, so each new one makes a BIG difference.

Your honest review is a big encouragement for us, new creators and sellers, to keep going. And it helps other people find our product, too!

(To leave a review go to the product page on Amazon, scroll down and select "Write a customer review")

Let's be friends! - CONNECT and SHARE with us

We would be thrilled to hear (read) about your journal ideas or other comments & suggestions you may have. And if you would like to be part of our "launch team" to receive free samples of future journal concepts, please let us know, too!

Instagram: @adaytoremember_journals
Amazon: follow "A Day to Remember Journals"
or email us at: adaytoremember.journals@gmail.com.

And please "tag us" on Instagram when you post about your experiences!
WE WOULD ♥ TO BE PART OF YOUR JOURNEY
the same way we feel that you are a BIG part of ours!

xoxo, Carla and Milena

How to use this Journal - Part 1

** Therapy Sessions Schedule **

Use this space to plan for your sessions in an organized way. Gradually fill in the date & time of the sessions, along with the name of your therapist and his/her contacts, address and/or some short note that you need to easily remember.

** Therapy Goals **

Here we encourage you to write your "big picture goals", those that you will be discussing over several therapy sessions. For example:
- improve a relationship / not allow a bad relationship to affect all areas of your life, or
- overcome drug addiction/depression, and so on.

We encourage you to write a date when that goal was established, and to also list some actions / things that could help - eg. exercising and reconnecting with friends.

** Therapy Tools I learned **

Therapy tools can help you throughout your journey.
Whenever you learn a tool capture it on this page so that you can easily refer back to it when you need it.

You may first write about the tool on the "insights page" of a therapy session (eg. when you learn about it from your therapist). But as soon as you have a feeling that a tool could help you in many occasions, you should also write the information on the "tools pages" for easy reference.

How to use this Journal - Part 2

Therapy Session Notes

Before each of your therapy sessions, try to read our suggestions and write down in the "Topics I want to discuss" area what you plan to talk about with or ask your therapist.

To get the most out of your sessions, help your therapist by coming prepared with your most pressing needs/questions.

During your discussion with the therapist, or as soon as possible afterwards, write down your main insights and takeaways from the session. Look back on these notes between sessions to see and sustain your progress.

** Check Up Pages **

After you have documented 4 or 5 therapy sessions (this journal assumes that you have sessions once a week and 4 or 5 in a month), you can make a check up/review on how things evolved during that period. This will help you notice small or large advances and help you feel motivated to continue.

** Meaningful Quotes & Thoughts Pages **

Do you know that quote or thought that moves you in some way and that you want to keep forever accessing? This page was designed for that. Write down the coolest quotes and thoughts that bring you good energy and feelings that can help your therapy process so that you can always revisit them here.

** Additional Notes pages **

Every time you have a thought or idea that you believe will be an important one to remember and go back to over time, write it down on the "Additional Notes pages". Capture the date and other relevant aspects related to your thought or idea.

You may also use this section if you need additional space to write before, during and after the therapy sessions (ie. as a continuation of Therapy Session Notes Section).

Let's get started!

Therapy Sessions Schedule

	DATE/TIME	THERAPIST	THERAPIST CONTACT	ADDRESS/ NOTE
SESSION 1				
SESSION 2				
SESSION 3				
SESSION 4				
SESSION 5				
SESSION 6				
SESSION 7				
SESSION 8				
SESSION 9				

	DATE/TIME	THERAPIST	THERAPIST CONTACT	ADDRESS/NOTE
SESSION 10				
SESSION 11				
SESSION 12				
SESSION 13				
SESSION 14				
SESSION 15				
SESSION 16				
SESSION 17				
SESSION 18				
SESSION 19				
SESSION 20				

	DATE/TIME	THERAPIST	THERAPIST CONTACT	ADDRESS/NOTE
SESSION 21				
SESSION 22				
SESSION 23				
SESSION 24				
SESSION 25				
SESSION 26				
SESSION 27				
SESSION 28				
SESSION 29				
SESSION 30				

Therapy Goals

Write your goal(s) for your therapy sessions and the actions you need to take to achieve them. (Come back and review your goals whenever is necessary. Eg: Every 2 months)

GOAL: Overcoming depression after a break up   **DATE:**

Example

ACTIONS:

I will start exercising again - 3 times a week at least, for 45 minutes each time

I will stop refusing my firends invitations to get together, I will socialize again

I will journal briefly every day, answering this: what are you proud of having done today?

GOAL: **DATE:**

ACTIONS:

GOAL: **DATE:**

ACTIONS:

GOAL: **DATE:**

ACTIONS:

Therapy Tools I Learned

Therapy tools can help you throughout your journey. Whenever you learn a tool capture it here so that you can easily refer back to it when you need it.

TOOL: *Journaling*

Example

DESCRIPTION / RELEVANT NOTES:

My therapist suggested that I write down the things that make me happy during the day. And also to write down when I feel confused and unable to make a decision.

I love this tool because I fell more relaxed and less anxious as I vent my thoughts. It also helps me to feel more focused and organized because I gain more clarity to prioritize what is really important to me.

TOOL: **DATE:**

DESCRIPTION / RELEVANT NOTES:

TOOL: **DATE:**

DESCRIPTION / RELEVANT NOTES:

TOOL: **DATE:**

DESCRIPTION / RELEVANT NOTES:

Therapy Sessions Notes
&
Suggestions Pages

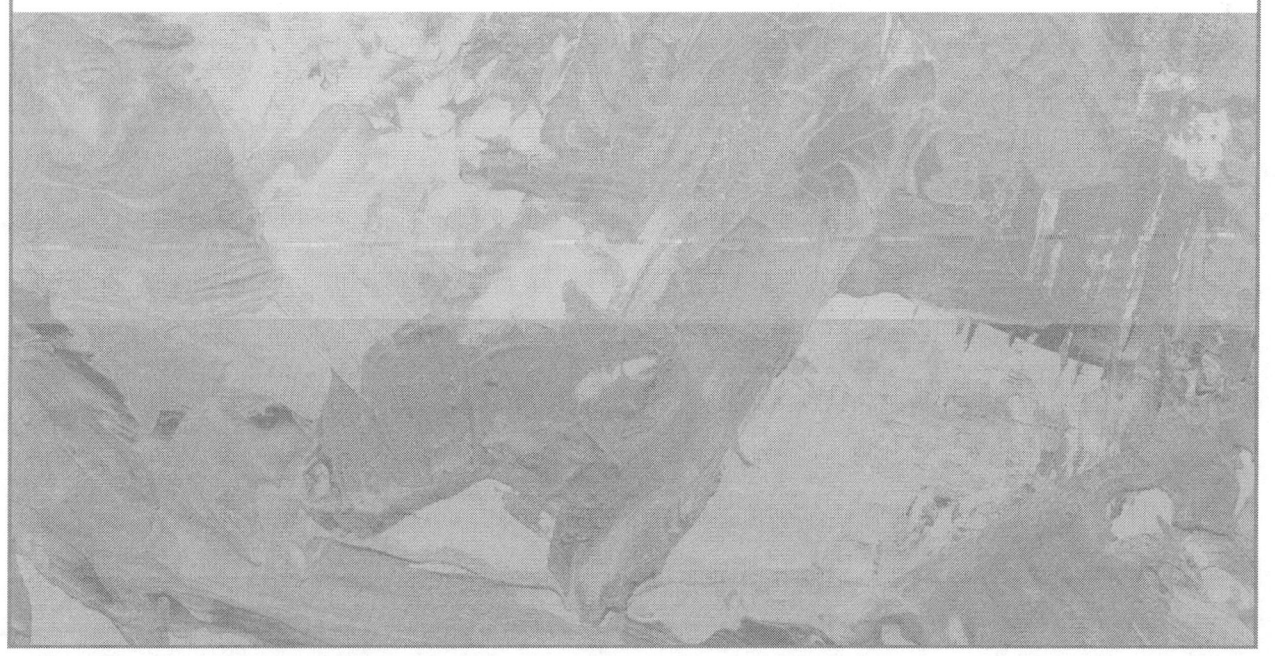

MONTH 1

Date:

Session: #

Next Session:

Mood Tracker

Before the Session:
Very Good — Neutral — Not great

After the Session:
Very Good — Neutral — Not great

Suggestions of things to think and write about:
(The prompts below will be the same for all the sessions because they can be a simple starting point for you to write, reflect and track your progress over time. Feel free to use them or write freely about your session)

- Topic(s) I want to discuss and goal(s) for the session.
  Reflection: How do they affect my life?

- How do I feel physically and emotionally after my session today? Any shifts in my breathing, heart rate, muscle tightness? Try to describe your thoughts and feelings.

- Did I feel heard and comfortable with my therapist today? Did I feel safe to communicate my needs and goals to her/him? Is our therapeutic relationship evolving?

- Do I already see ways to help myself to get over my symptoms and reach my goals?

- How can I use the takeaways from this session to help me with my therapy process and improve my life?

- Write about possible actions, tools you learned and follow ups from the therapist.

My Notes (from before, during and/or after session).
If you need more space, please use the Additional Notes Section at the end of this journal

....
....
....
....
....
....
....

....
....
....
....
....
....
....
....
....
....
....
....
....
....

The main things that I want to remember from today are:

(Some ideas: Homework, key takeaways, reminders for your next session, challenges to keep in mind and wins to be celebrated!)

-
-
-

MONTH 1

Date:

Session: #

Next Session:

Mood Tracker

Before the Session:

Very Good — Neutral — Not great

After the Session:

Very Good — Neutral — Not great

Suggestions of things to think and write about:
(The prompts below will be the same for all the sessions because they can be a simple starting point for you to write, reflect and track your progress over time. Feel free to use them or write freely about your session)

✎ Topic(s) I want to discuss and goal(s) for the session.
   Reflection: How do they affect my life?

✎ How do I feel physically and emotionally after my session today? Any shifts in my breathing, heart rate, muscle tightness? Try to describe your thoughts and feelings.

✎ Did I feel heard and comfortable with my therapist today? Did I feel safe to communicate my needs and goals to her/him? Is our therapeutic relationship evolving?

✎ Do I already see ways to help myself to get over my symptoms and reach my goals?

✎ How can I use the takeaways from this session to help me with my therapy process and improve my life?

✎ Write about possible actions, tools you learned and follow ups from the therapist.

My Notes (from before, during and/or after session).
If you need more space, please use the Additional Notes Section at the end of this journal

....

....

....

....

....

....

The main things that I want to remember from today are:

(Some ideas: Homework, key takeaways, reminders for your next session, challenges to keep in mind and wins to be celebrated!)

MONTH 1

Date: **Session: #**

Next Session:

Mood Tracker
Before the Session:

Very Good   Neutral   Not great

After the Session:

Very Good   Neutral   Not great

Suggestions of things to think and write about:
(The prompts below will be the same for all the sessions because they can be a simple starting point for you to write, reflect and track your progress over time. Feel free to use them or write freely about your session)

- Topic(s) I want to discuss and goal(s) for the session.
  Reflection: How do they affect my life?

- How do I feel physically and emotionally after my session today? Any shifts in my breathing, heart rate, muscle tightness? Try to describe your thoughts and feelings.

- Did I feel heard and comfortable with my therapist today? Did I feel safe to communicate my needs and goals to her/him? Is our therapeutic relationship evolving?

- Do I already see ways to help myself to get over my symptoms and reach my goals?

- How can I use the takeaways from this session to help me with my therapy process and improve my life?

- Write about possible actions, tools you learned and follow ups from the therapist.

My Notes (from before, during and/or after session).
If you need more space, please use the Additional Notes Section at the end of this journal

....

....

....

....

....

....

The main things that I want to remember from today are:

(Some ideas: Homework, key takeaways, reminders for your next session, challenges to keep in mind and wins to be celebrated!)

-
-
-

MONTH 1

Date:

Session: #

Next Session:

Mood Tracker

Before the Session:
Very Good — Neutral — Not great

After the Session:
Very Good — Neutral — Not great

Suggestions of things to think and write about:
(The prompts below will be the same for all the sessions because they can be a simple starting point for you to write, reflect and track your progress over time. Feel free to use them or write freely about your session)

- Topic(s) I want to discuss and goal(s) for the session.
  Reflection: How do they affect my life?

- How do I feel physically and emotionally after my session today? Any shifts in my breathing, heart rate, muscle tightness? Try to describe your thoughts and feelings.

- Did I feel heard and comfortable with my therapist today? Did I feel safe to communicate my needs and goals to her/him? Is our therapeutic relationship evolving?

- Do I already see ways to help myself to get over my symptoms and reach my goals?

- How can I use the takeaways from this session to help me with my therapy process and improve my life?

- Write about possible actions, tools you learned and follow ups from the therapist.

My Notes (from before, during and/or after session).
If you need more space, please use the Additional Notes Section at the end of this journal

....

....

....

....

....

....

....
....
....
....
....
....
....
....
....
....
....
....
....
....

The main things that I want to remember from today are:

(Some ideas: Homework, key takeaways, reminders for your next session, challenges to keep in mind and wins to be celebrated!)

-
-
-

MONTH 1

Date:

Session: #

Next Session:

Mood Tracker

Before the Session:
Very Good — Neutral — Not great

After the Session:
Very Good — Neutral — Not great

Suggestions of things to think and write about:
(The prompts below will be the same for all the sessions because they can be a simple starting point for you to write, reflect and track your progress over time. Feel free to use them or write freely about your session)

- Topic(s) I want to discuss and goal(s) for the session.
  Reflection: How do they affect my life?

- How do I feel physically and emotionally after my session today? Any shifts in my breathing, heart rate, muscle tightness? Try to describe your thoughts and feelings.

- Did I feel heard and comfortable with my therapist today? Did I feel safe to communicate my needs and goals to her/him? Is our therapeutic relationship evolving?

- Do I already see ways to help myself to get over my symptoms and reach my goals?

- How can I use the takeaways from this session to help me with my therapy process and improve my life?

- Write about possible actions, tools you learned and follow ups from the therapist.

My Notes (from before, during and/or after session).
If you need more space, please use the Additional Notes Section at the end of this journal

....

....

....

....

....

....

....
....
....
....
....
....
....
....
....
....
....
....
....
....

The main things that I want to remember from today are:

(Some ideas: Homework, key takeaways, reminders for your next session, challenges to keep in mind and wins to be celebrated!)

-
-
-

✓ 30 Days Check Up ✓

MONTH 1

Monthly Progress Tracker:

Beginning of the first Month:		End of the first Month:	
How do I feel physically? (In a scale 1 - 5, with 5 being the best)	☐☐☐☐☐	**How do I feel physically now?** (In a scale 1 - 5, with 5 being the best)	☐☐☐☐☐
How do I feel emotionally? (In a scale 1 - 5, with 5 being the best)	☐☐☐☐☐	**How do I feel emotionally now?** (In a scale 1 - 5, with 5 being the best)	☐☐☐☐☐
How is the quality of my sleep? (In a scale 1 - 5, with 5 being the best)	☐☐☐☐☐	**How is the quality of my sleep now?** (In a scale 1 - 5, with 5 being the best)	☐☐☐☐☐
Overall Mood/wellbeing: (In a scale 1 - 5, with 5 being the best)	☐☐☐☐☐	**Overall mood/wellbeing now:** (In a scale 1 - 5, with 5 being the best)	☐☐☐☐☐

How helpful these sessions were? Which were the most important sessions of the month? Why was that?

How do I evaluate my interaction with my therapist? Do I feel heard and embraced? What are the most valuable tools he/she has given me this month to work with?

Did I notice any changes or shifts during this month? If yes, what may have contributed to the changes? What do I notice feeling now?

Important takeaways and reminders for the next month sessions (from me & from my therapist):

Meaningful Quotes & Thoughts

*My Therapist always says that Feelings need to be acknowledge.
They don't just go away if I ignore them.
I'm allowed to feel everything I need and then release it.*

MONTH 2

Date:

Session: #

Next Session:

Mood Tracker

Before the Session:
Very Good — Neutral — Not great

After the Session:
Very Good — Neutral — Not great

Suggestions of things to think and write about:
(The prompts below will be the same for all the sessions because they can be a simple starting point for you to write, reflect and track your progress over time. Feel free to use them or write freely about your session)

✏️ Topic(s) I want to discuss and goal(s) for the session.
Reflection: How do they affect my life?

✏️ How do I feel physically and emotionally after my session today? Any shifts in my breathing, heart rate, muscle tightness? Try to describe your thoughts and feelings.

✏️ Did I feel heard and comfortable with my therapist today? Did I feel safe to communicate my needs and goals to her/him? Is our therapeutic relationship evolving?

✏️ Do I already see ways to help myself to get over my symptoms and reach my goals?

✏️ How can I use the takeaways from this session to help me with my therapy process and improve my life?

✏️ Write about possible actions, tools you learned and follow ups from the therapist.

My Notes (from before, during and/or after session).
If you need more space, please use the Additional Notes Section at the end of this journal

....
....
....
....
....
....
....

The main things that I want to remember from today are:

(Some ideas: Homework, key takeaways, reminders for your next session, challenges to keep in mind and wins to be celebrated!)

-
-
-

MONTH 2

Date:

Session: #

Next Session:

Mood Tracker

Before the Session:

Very Good — Neutral — Not great

After the Session:

Very Good — Neutral — Not great

Suggestions of things to think and write about:
(The prompts below will be the same for all the sessions because they can be a simple starting point for you to write, reflect and track your progress over time. Feel free to use them or write freely about your session)

- Topic(s) I want to discuss and goal(s) for the session.
  Reflection: How do they affect my life?

- How do I feel physically and emotionally after my session today? Any shifts in my breathing, heart rate, muscle tightness? Try to describe your thoughts and feelings.

- Did I feel heard and comfortable with my therapist today? Did I feel safe to communicate my needs and goals to her/him? Is our therapeutic relationship evolving?

- Do I already see ways to help myself to get over my symptoms and reach my goals?

- How can I use the takeaways from this session to help me with my therapy process and improve my life?

- Write about possible actions, tools you learned and follow ups from the therapist.

My Notes (from before, during and/or after session).
If you need more space, please use the Additional Notes Section at the end of this journal

....

....

....

....

....

....

....
....
....
....
....
....
....
....
....
....
....
....
....

The main things that I want to remember from today are:

(Some ideas: Homework, key takeaways, reminders for your next session, challenges to keep in mind and wins to be celebrated!)

-
-
-

MONTH 2

Date:　　　　　　　　**Session: #**

Next Session:

Mood Tracker

Before the Session:　　　　After the Session:

Very Good　Neutral　Not great　　Very Good　Neutral　Not great

Suggestions of things to think and write about:
(The prompts below will be the same for all the sessions because they can be a simple starting point for you to write, reflect and track your progress over time. Feel free to use them or write freely about your session)

✎ Topic(s) I want to discuss and goal(s) for the session.
　Reflection: How do they affect my life?

✎ How do I feel physically and emotionally after my session today? Any shifts in my breathing, heart rate, muscle tightness? Try to describe your thoughts and feelings.

✎ Did I feel heard and comfortable with my therapist today? Did I feel safe to communicate my needs and goals to her/him? Is our therapeutic relationship evolving?

✎ Do I already see ways to help myself to get over my symptoms and reach my goals?

✎ How can I use the takeaways from this session to help me with my therapy process and improve my life?

✎ Write about possible actions, tools you learned and follow ups from the therapist.

My Notes (from before, during and/or after session).
If you need more space, please use the Additional Notes Section at the end of this journal

....

....

....

....

....

....

The main things that I want to remember from today are:

(Some ideas: Homework, key takeaways, reminders for your next session, challenges to keep in mind and wins to be celebrated!)

MONTH 2

Date: **Session: #**

Next Session:

Mood Tracker

Before the Session: | After the Session:

Very Good — Neutral — Not great | Very Good — Neutral — Not great

Suggestions of things to think and write about:
(The prompts below will be the same for all the sessions because they can be a simple starting point for you to write, reflect and track your progress over time. Feel free to use them or write freely about your session)

✏️ Topic(s) I want to discuss and goal(s) for the session.
Reflection: How do they affect my life?

✏️ How do I feel physically and emotionally after my session today? Any shifts in my breathing, heart rate, muscle tightness? Try to describe your thoughts and feelings.

✏️ Did I feel heard and comfortable with my therapist today? Did I feel safe to communicate my needs and goals to her/him? Is our therapeutic relationship evolving?

✏️ Do I already see ways to help myself to get over my symptoms and reach my goals?

✏️ How can I use the takeaways from this session to help me with my therapy process and improve my life?

✏️ Write about possible actions, tools you learned and follow ups from the therapist.

My Notes (from before, during and/or after session).
If you need more space, please use the Additional Notes Section at the end of this journal

....

....

....

....

....

....

....
....
....
....
....
....
....
....
....
....
....
....
....
....

The main things that I want to remember from today are:

(Some ideas: Homework, key takeaways, reminders for your next session, challenges to keep in mind and wins to be celebrated!)

-
-
-

MONTH 2

Date: **Session: #**

Next Session:

Mood Tracker

Before the Session: After the Session:

Very Good   Neutral   Not great   Very Good   Neutral   Not great

Suggestions of things to think and write about:
(The prompts below will be the same for all the sessions because they can be a simple starting point for you to write, reflect and track your progress over time. Feel free to use them or write freely about your session)

- Topic(s) I want to discuss and goal(s) for the session.
  Reflection: How do they affect my life?

- How do I feel physically and emotionally after my session today? Any shifts in my breathing, heart rate, muscle tightness? Try to describe your thoughts and feelings.

- Did I feel heard and comfortable with my therapist today? Did I feel safe to communicate my needs and goals to her/him? Is our therapeutic relationship evolving?

- Do I already see ways to help myself to get over my symptoms and reach my goals?

- How can I use the takeaways from this session to help me with my therapy process and improve my life?

- Write about possible actions, tools you learned and follow ups from the therapist.

My Notes (from before, during and/or after session).
If you need more space, please use the Additional Notes Section at the end of this journal

....

....

....

....

....

....

The main things that I want to remember from today are:

(Some ideas: Homework, key takeaways, reminders for your next session, challenges to keep in mind and wins to be celebrated!)

-
-
-

30 Days Check Up

MONTH 2

Monthly Progress Tracker:

Beginning of the first Month:	End of the first Month:
How do I feel physically? (In a scale 1 - 5, with 5 being the best) ☐☐☐☐☐	**How do I feel physically now?** (In a scale 1 - 5, with 5 being the best) ☐☐☐☐☐
How do I feel emotionally? (In a scale 1 - 5, with 5 being the best) ☐☐☐☐☐	**How do I feel emotionally now?** (In a scale 1 - 5, with 5 being the best) ☐☐☐☐☐
How is the quality of my sleep? (In a scale 1 - 5, with 5 being the best) ☐☐☐☐☐	**How is the quality of my sleep now?** (In a scale 1 - 5, with 5 being the best) ☐☐☐☐☐
Overall Mood/wellbeing: (In a scale 1 - 5, with 5 being the best) ☐☐☐☐☐	**Overall mood/wellbeing now:** (In a scale 1 - 5, with 5 being the best) ☐☐☐☐☐

How helpful these sessions were? Which were the most important sessions of the month? Why was that?

How do I evaluate my interaction with my therapist? Do I feel heard and embraced? What are the most valuable tools he/she has given me this month to work with?

Did I notice any changes or shifts during this month? If yes, what may have contributed to the changes? What do I notice feeling now?

Important takeaways and reminders for the next month sessions (from me & from my therapist):

Meaningful Quotes & Thoughts

Make a conscious effort to do things that maintain, improve and repair your mental, emotional, physical and spiritual wellness.

MONTH 3

Date:

Session: #

Next Session:

Mood Tracker

Before the Session:

Very Good — Neutral — Not great

After the Session:

Very Good — Neutral — Not great

Suggestions of things to think and write about:
(The prompts below will be the same for all the sessions because they can be a simple starting point for you to write, reflect and track your progress over time. Feel free to use them or write freely about your session)

- Topic(s) I want to discuss and goal(s) for the session.
  Reflection: How do they affect my life?

- How do I feel physically and emotionally after my session today? Any shifts in my breathing, heart rate, muscle tightness? Try to describe your thoughts and feelings.

- Did I feel heard and comfortable with my therapist today? Did I feel safe to communicate my needs and goals to her/him? Is our therapeutic relationship evolving?

- Do I already see ways to help myself to get over my symptoms and reach my goals?

- How can I use the takeaways from this session to help me with my therapy process and improve my life?

- Write about possible actions, tools you learned and follow ups from the therapist.

My Notes (from before, during and/or after session).
If you need more space, please use the Additional Notes Section at the end of this journal

....

....

....

....

....

....
....
....
....
....
....
....
....
....
....
....
....
....
....

The main things that I want to remember from today are:

(Some ideas: Homework, key takeaways, reminders for your next session, challenges to keep in mind and wins to be celebrated!)

-
-
-

MONTH 3

Date: **Session: #**

Next Session:

Mood Tracker
Before the Session: | After the Session:
Very Good — Neutral — Not great | Very Good — Neutral — Not great

Suggestions of things to think and write about:
(The prompts below will be the same for all the sessions because they can be a simple starting point for you to write, reflect and track your progress over time. Feel free to use them or write freely about your session)

- ✎ Topic(s) I want to discuss and goal(s) for the session.
  Reflection: How do they affect my life?

- ✎ How do I feel physically and emotionally after my session today? Any shifts in my breathing, heart rate, muscle tightness? Try to describe your thoughts and feelings.

- ✎ Did I feel heard and comfortable with my therapist today? Did I feel safe to communicate my needs and goals to her/him? Is our therapeutic relationship evolving?

- ✎ Do I already see ways to help myself to get over my symptoms and reach my goals?

- ✎ How can I use the takeaways from this session to help me with my therapy process and improve my life?

- ✎ Write about possible actions, tools you learned and follow ups from the therapist.

My Notes (from before, during and/or after session).
If you need more space, please use the Additional Notes Section at the end of this journal

....
....
....
....
....
....

....
....
....
....
....
....
....
....
....
....
....
....
....
....
....

The main things that I want to remember from today are:

(Some ideas: Homework, key takeaways, reminders for your next session, challenges to keep in mind and wins to be celebrated!)

-
-
-

MONTH 3

Date: **Session: #**

Next Session:

Mood Tracker
Before the Session: | After the Session:

Very Good — Neutral — Not great | Very Good — Neutral — Not great

Suggestions of things to think and write about:
(The prompts below will be the same for all the sessions because they can be a simple starting point for you to write, reflect and track your progress over time. Feel free to use them or write freely about your session)

- Topic(s) I want to discuss and goal(s) for the session.
  Reflection: How do they affect my life?

- How do I feel physically and emotionally after my session today? Any shifts in my breathing, heart rate, muscle tightness? Try to describe your thoughts and feelings.

- Did I feel heard and comfortable with my therapist today? Did I feel safe to communicate my needs and goals to her/him? Is our therapeutic relationship evolving?

- Do I already see ways to help myself to get over my symptoms and reach my goals?

- How can I use the takeaways from this session to help me with my therapy process and improve my life?

- Write about possible actions, tools you learned and follow ups from the therapist.

My Notes (from before, during and/or after session).
If you need more space, please use the Additional Notes Section at the end of this journal

....

....

....

....

....

....

....
....
....
....
....
....
....
....
....
....
....
....
....
....

The main things that I want to remember from today are:

(Some ideas: Homework, key takeaways, reminders for your next session, challenges to keep in mind and wins to be celebrated!)

-
-
-

MONTH 3

Date:

Session: #

Next Session:

Mood Tracker

Before the Session:
Very Good — Neutral — Not great

After the Session:
Very Good — Neutral — Not great

Suggestions of things to think and write about:
(The prompts below will be the same for all the sessions because they can be a simple starting point for you to write, reflect and track your progress over time. Feel free to use them or write freely about your session)

- Topic(s) I want to discuss and goal(s) for the session.
  Reflection: How do they affect my life?

- How do I feel physically and emotionally after my session today? Any shifts in my breathing, heart rate, muscle tightness? Try to describe your thoughts and feelings.

- Did I feel heard and comfortable with my therapist today? Did I feel safe to communicate my needs and goals to her/him? Is our therapeutic relationship evolving?

- Do I already see ways to help myself to get over my symptoms and reach my goals?

- How can I use the takeaways from this session to help me with my therapy process and improve my life?

- Write about possible actions, tools you learned and follow ups from the therapist.

My Notes (from before, during and/or after session).
If you need more space, please use the Additional Notes Section at the end of this journal

....

....

....

....

....

....

The main things that I want to remember from today are:

(Some ideas: Homework, key takeaways, reminders for your next session, challenges to keep in mind and wins to be celebrated!)

-
-
-

MONTH 3

Date:

Session: #

Next Session:

Mood Tracker

Before the Session:

Very Good — Neutral — Not great

After the Session:

Very Good — Neutral — Not great

Suggestions of things to think and write about:
(The prompts below will be the same for all the sessions because they can be a simple starting point for you to write, reflect and track your progress over time. Feel free to use them or write freely about your session)

- Topic(s) I want to discuss and goal(s) for the session.
  Reflection: How do they affect my life?

- How do I feel physically and emotionally after my session today? Any shifts in my breathing, heart rate, muscle tightness? Try to describe your thoughts and feelings.

- Did I feel heard and comfortable with my therapist today? Did I feel safe to communicate my needs and goals to her/him? Is our therapeutic relationship evolving?

- Do I already see ways to help myself to get over my symptoms and reach my goals?

- How can I use the takeaways from this session to help me with my therapy process and improve my life?

- Write about possible actions, tools you learned and follow ups from the therapist.

My Notes (from before, during and/or after session).
If you need more space, please use the Additional Notes Section at the end of this journal

....
....
....
....
....
....
....
....
....
....
....
....
....
....

The main things that I want to remember from today are:

(Some ideas: Homework, key takeaways, reminders for your next session, challenges to keep in mind and wins to be celebrated!)

-
-
-

✓ 30 Days Check Up ✓

Monthly Progress Tracker:

MONTH 3

Beginning of the first Month:		End of the first Month:	
How do I feel physically? (In a scale 1 - 5, with 5 being the best)	☐☐☐☐☐	**How do I feel physically now?** (In a scale 1 - 5, with 5 being the best)	☐☐☐☐☐
How do I feel emotionally? (In a scale 1 - 5, with 5 being the best)	☐☐☐☐☐	**How do I feel emotionally now?** (In a scale 1 - 5, with 5 being the best)	☐☐☐☐☐
How is the quality of my sleep? (In a scale 1 - 5, with 5 being the best)	☐☐☐☐☐	**How is the quality of my sleep now?** (In a scale 1 - 5, with 5 being the best)	☐☐☐☐☐
Overall Mood/wellbeing: (In a scale 1 - 5, with 5 being the best)	☐☐☐☐☐	**Overall mood/wellbeing now:** (In a scale 1 - 5, with 5 being the best)	☐☐☐☐☐

How helpful these sessions were? Which were the most important sessions of the month? Why was that?

How do I evaluate my interaction with my therapist? Do I feel heard and embraced? What are the most valuable tools he/she has given me this month to work with?

Did I notice any changes or shifts during this month? If yes, what may have contributed to the changes? What do I notice feeling now?

Important takeaways and reminders for the next month sessions (from me & from my therapist):

Meaningful Quotes & Thoughts

Especially if you're feeling vulnerable, sad, alone or triggered by something, talking to people about your experiences and feelings is very important.
You are not alone!

MONTH 4

Date:

Session: #

Next Session:

Mood Tracker

Before the Session:
Very Good — Neutral — Not great

After the Session:
Very Good — Neutral — Not great

Suggestions of things to think and write about:
(The prompts below will be the same for all the sessions because they can be a simple starting point for you to write, reflect and track your progress over time. Feel free to use them or write freely about your session)

✎ Topic(s) I want to discuss and goal(s) for the session.
Reflection: How do they affect my life?

✎ How do I feel physically and emotionally after my session today? Any shifts in my breathing, heart rate, muscle tightness? Try to describe your thoughts and feelings.

✎ Did I feel heard and comfortable with my therapist today? Did I feel safe to communicate my needs and goals to her/him? Is our therapeutic relationship evolving?

✎ Do I already see ways to help myself to get over my symptoms and reach my goals?

✎ How can I use the takeaways from this session to help me with my therapy process and improve my life?

✎ Write about possible actions, tools you learned and follow ups from the therapist.

My Notes (from before, during and/or after session).
If you need more space, please use the Additional Notes Section at the end of this journal

....

....

....

....

....

....

....
....
....
....
....
....
....
....
....
....
....
....
....
....

The main things that I want to remember from today are:

(Some ideas: Homework, key takeaways, reminders for your next session, challenges to keep in mind and wins to be celebrated!)

-
-
-

MONTH 4

Date:

Session: #

Next Session:

Mood Tracker

Before the Session:
Very Good — Neutral — Not great

After the Session:
Very Good — Neutral — Not great

Suggestions of things to think and write about:
(The prompts below will be the same for all the sessions because they can be a simple starting point for you to write, reflect and track your progress over time. Feel free to use them or write freely about your session)

- **Topic(s) I want to discuss and goal(s) for the session. Reflection: How do they affect my life?**

- **How do I feel physically and emotionally after my session today? Any shifts in my breathing, heart rate, muscle tightness? Try to describe your thoughts and feelings.**

- **Did I feel heard and comfortable with my therapist today? Did I feel safe to communicate my needs and goals to her/him? Is our therapeutic relationship evolving?**

- **Do I already see ways to help myself to get over my symptoms and reach my goals?**

- **How can I use the takeaways from this session to help me with my therapy process and improve my life?**

- **Write about possible actions, tools you learned and follow ups from the therapist.**

My Notes (from before, during and/or after session).
If you need more space, please use the Additional Notes Section at the end of this journal

....
....
....
....
....
....
....

The main things that I want to remember from today are:

(Some ideas: Homework, key takeaways, reminders for your next session, challenges to keep in mind and wins to be celebrated!)

-
-
-

MONTH 4

Date:

Session: #

Next Session:

Mood Tracker

Before the Session:
Very Good — Neutral — Not great

After the Session:
Very Good — Neutral — Not great

Suggestions of things to think and write about:
(The prompts below will be the same for all the sessions because they can be a simple starting point for you to write, reflect and track your progress over time. Feel free to use them or write freely about your session)

- **Topic(s) I want to discuss and goal(s) for the session. Reflection: How do they affect my life?**

- **How do I feel physically and emotionally after my session today? Any shifts in my breathing, heart rate, muscle tightness? Try to describe your thoughts and feelings.**

- **Did I feel heard and comfortable with my therapist today? Did I feel safe to communicate my needs and goals to her/him? Is our therapeutic relationship evolving?**

- **Do I already see ways to help myself to get over my symptoms and reach my goals?**

- **How can I use the takeaways from this session to help me with my therapy process and improve my life?**

- **Write about possible actions, tools you learned and follow ups from the therapist.**

My Notes (from before, during and/or after session).
If you need more space, please use the Additional Notes Section at the end of this journal

The main things that I want to remember from today are:

(Some ideas: Homework, key takeaways, reminders for your next session, challenges to keep in mind and wins to be celebrated!)

MONTH 4

Date:

Session: #

Next Session:

Mood Tracker

Before the Session:
Very Good — Neutral — Not great

After the Session:
Very Good — Neutral — Not great

Suggestions of things to think and write about:
(The prompts below will be the same for all the sessions because they can be a simple starting point for you to write, reflect and track your progress over time. Feel free to use them or write freely about your session)

- **Topic(s) I want to discuss and goal(s) for the session. Reflection: How do they affect my life?**

- **How do I feel physically and emotionally after my session today? Any shifts in my breathing, heart rate, muscle tightness? Try to describe your thoughts and feelings.**

- **Did I feel heard and comfortable with my therapist today? Did I feel safe to communicate my needs and goals to her/him? Is our therapeutic relationship evolving?**

- **Do I already see ways to help myself to get over my symptoms and reach my goals?**

- **How can I use the takeaways from this session to help me with my therapy process and improve my life?**

- **Write about possible actions, tools you learned and follow ups from the therapist.**

My Notes (from before, during and/or after session).
If you need more space, please use the Additional Notes Section at the end of this journal

....

....

....

....

....

....

....
....
....
....
....
....
....
....
....
....
....
....
....
....

The main things that I want to remember from today are:

(Some ideas: Homework, key takeaways, reminders for your next session, challenges to keep in mind and wins to be celebrated!)

-
-
-

MONTH 4

Date:

Session: #

Next Session:

Mood Tracker

Before the Session:
Very Good — Neutral — Not great

After the Session:
Very Good — Neutral — Not great

Suggestions of things to think and write about:
(The prompts below will be the same for all the sessions because they can be a simple starting point for you to write, reflect and track your progress over time. Feel free to use them or write freely about your session)

- **Topic(s) I want to discuss and goal(s) for the session.**
  Reflection: How do they affect my life?

- **How do I feel physically and emotionally after my session today? Any shifts in my breathing, heart rate, muscle tightness? Try to describe your thoughts and feelings.**

- **Did I feel heard and comfortable with my therapist today? Did I feel safe to communicate my needs and goals to her/him? Is our therapeutic relationship evolving?**

- **Do I already see ways to help myself to get over my symptoms and reach my goals?**

- **How can I use the takeaways from this session to help me with my therapy process and improve my life?**

- **Write about possible actions, tools you learned and follow ups from the therapist.**

My Notes (from before, during and/or after session).
If you need more space, please use the Additional Notes Section at the end of this journal

....

....

....

....

....

....

....
....
....
....
....
....
....
....
....
....
....
....
....
....

The main things that I want to remember from today are:

(Some ideas: Homework, key takeaways, reminders for your next session, challenges to keep in mind and wins to be celebrated!)

-
-
-

30 Days Check Up

Monthly Progress Tracker:

MONTH 4

Beginning of the first Month:		End of the first Month:	
How do I feel physically? (In a scale 1 - 5, with 5 being the best)	☐☐☐☐☐	How do I feel physically now? (In a scale 1 - 5, with 5 being the best)	☐☐☐☐☐
How do I feel emotionally? (In a scale 1 - 5, with 5 being the best)	☐☐☐☐☐	How do I feel emotionally now? (In a scale 1 - 5, with 5 being the best)	☐☐☐☐☐
How is the quality of my sleep? (In a scale 1 - 5, with 5 being the best)	☐☐☐☐☐	How is the quality of my sleep now? (In a scale 1 - 5, with 5 being the best)	☐☐☐☐☐
Overall Mood/wellbeing: (In a scale 1 - 5, with 5 being the best)	☐☐☐☐☐	Overall mood/wellbeing now: (In a scale 1 - 5, with 5 being the best)	☐☐☐☐☐

How helpful these sessions were? Which were the most important sessions of the month? Why was that?

How do I evaluate my interaction with my therapist? Do I feel heard and embraced? What are the most valuable tools he/she has given me this month to work with?

Did I notice any changes or shifts during this month? If yes, what may have contributed to the changes? What do I notice feeling now?

Important takeaways and reminders for the next month sessions (from me & from my therapist):

Meaningful Quotes & Thoughts

"The greatest discovery of my generation is that human beings can alter their lives by altering their attitudes of mind."
William James

MONTH 5

Date:

Session: #

Next Session:

Mood Tracker

Before the Session:
Very Good — Neutral — Not great

After the Session:
Very Good — Neutral — Not great

Suggestions of things to think and write about:
(The prompts below will be the same for all the sessions because they can be a simple starting point for you to write, reflect and track your progress over time. Feel free to use them or write freely about your session)

- **Topic(s) I want to discuss and goal(s) for the session.**
  Reflection: How do they affect my life?

- **How do I feel physically and emotionally after my session today? Any shifts in my breathing, heart rate, muscle tightness? Try to describe your thoughts and feelings.**

- **Did I feel heard and comfortable with my therapist today? Did I feel safe to communicate my needs and goals to her/him? Is our therapeutic relationship evolving?**

- **Do I already see ways to help myself to get over my symptoms and reach my goals?**

- **How can I use the takeaways from this session to help me with my therapy process and improve my life?**

- **Write about possible actions, tools you learned and follow ups from the therapist.**

My Notes (from before, during and/or after session).
If you need more space, please use the Additional Notes Section at the end of this journal

The main things that I want to remember from today are:

(Some ideas: Homework, key takeaways, reminders for your next session, challenges to keep in mind and wins to be celebrated!)

-
-
-

MONTH 5

Date:

Session: #

Next Session:

Mood Tracker

Before the Session:
Very Good — Neutral — Not great

After the Session:
Very Good — Neutral — Not great

Suggestions of things to think and write about:
(The prompts below will be the same for all the sessions because they can be a simple starting point for you to write, reflect and track your progress over time. Feel free to use them or write freely about your session)

- **Topic(s) I want to discuss and goal(s) for the session.**
  Reflection: How do they affect my life?

- **How do I feel physically and emotionally after my session today? Any shifts in my breathing, heart rate, muscle tightness? Try to describe your thoughts and feelings.**

- **Did I feel heard and comfortable with my therapist today? Did I feel safe to communicate my needs and goals to her/him? Is our therapeutic relationship evolving?**

- **Do I already see ways to help myself to get over my symptoms and reach my goals?**

- **How can I use the takeaways from this session to help me with my therapy process and improve my life?**

- **Write about possible actions, tools you learned and follow ups from the therapist.**

My Notes (from before, during and/or after session).
If you need more space, please use the Additional Notes Section at the end of this journal

....

....

....

....

....

....

The main things that I want to remember from today are:

(Some ideas: Homework, key takeaways, reminders for your next session, challenges to keep in mind and wins to be celebrated!)

-
-
-

MONTH 5

Date:

Session: #

Next Session:

Mood Tracker

Before the Session:
Very Good — Neutral — Not great

After the Session:
Very Good — Neutral — Not great

Suggestions of things to think and write about:
(The prompts below will be the same for all the sessions because they can be a simple starting point for you to write, reflect and track your progress over time. Feel free to use them or write freely about your session)

- **Topic(s) I want to discuss and goal(s) for the session.**
  Reflection: How do they affect my life?

- **How do I feel physically and emotionally after my session today? Any shifts in my breathing, heart rate, muscle tightness? Try to describe your thoughts and feelings.**

- **Did I feel heard and comfortable with my therapist today? Did I feel safe to communicate my needs and goals to her/him? Is our therapeutic relationship evolving?**

- **Do I already see ways to help myself to get over my symptoms and reach my goals?**

- **How can I use the takeaways from this session to help me with my therapy process and improve my life?**

- **Write about possible actions, tools you learned and follow ups from the therapist.**

My Notes (from before, during and/or after session).
If you need more space, please use the Additional Notes Section at the end of this journal

....

....

....

....

....

....

....

....

....

....

....

....

....

....

....

....

....

....

....

....

The main things that I want to remember from today are:

(Some ideas: Homework, key takeaways, reminders for your next session, challenges to keep in mind and wins to be celebrated!)

-
-
-

MONTH 5

Date:

Session: #

Next Session:

Mood Tracker

Before the Session:

😵 😢 🙂 😐 😒 😫

Very Good — Neutral — Not great

After the Session:

😵 😢 🙂 😐 😒 😫

Very Good — Neutral — Not great

Suggestions of things to think and write about:
(The prompts below will be the same for all the sessions because they can be a simple starting point for you to write, reflect and track your progress over time. Feel free to use them or write freely about your session)

✎ **Topic(s) I want to discuss and goal(s) for the session.**
Reflection: How do they affect my life?

✎ **How do I feel physically and emotionally after my session today? Any shifts in my breathing, heart rate, muscle tightness? Try to describe your thoughts and feelings.**

✎ **Did I feel heard and comfortable with my therapist today? Did I feel safe to communicate my needs and goals to her/him? Is our therapeutic relationship evolving?**

✎ **Do I already see ways to help myself to get over my symptoms and reach my goals?**

✎ **How can I use the takeaways from this session to help me with my therapy process and improve my life?**

✎ **Write about possible actions, tools you learned and follow ups from the therapist.**

My Notes (from before, during and/or after session).
If you need more space, please use the Additional Notes Section at the end of this journal

....

....

....

....

....

....

The main things that I want to remember from today are:

(Some ideas: Homework, key takeaways, reminders for your next session, challenges to keep in mind and wins to be celebrated!)

MONTH 5

Date:

Session: #

Next Session:

Mood Tracker

Before the Session:
Very Good — Neutral — Not great

After the Session:
Very Good — Neutral — Not great

Suggestions of things to think and write about:
(The prompts below will be the same for all the sessions because they can be a simple starting point for you to write, reflect and track your progress over time. Feel free to use them or write freely about your session)

- Topic(s) I want to discuss and goal(s) for the session.
  Reflection: How do they affect my life?

- How do I feel physically and emotionally after my session today? Any shifts in my breathing, heart rate, muscle tightness? Try to describe your thoughts and feelings.

- Did I feel heard and comfortable with my therapist today? Did I feel safe to communicate my needs and goals to her/him? Is our therapeutic relationship evolving?

- Do I already see ways to help myself to get over my symptoms and reach my goals?

- How can I use the takeaways from this session to help me with my therapy process and improve my life?

- Write about possible actions, tools you learned and follow ups from the therapist.

My Notes (from before, during and/or after session).
If you need more space, please use the Additional Notes Section at the end of this journal

....

....

....

....

....

....

....
....
....
....
....
....
....
....
....
....
....
....
....
....

The main things that I want to remember from today are:

(Some ideas: Homework, key takeaways, reminders for your next session, challenges to keep in mind and wins to be celebrated!)

-
-
-

✓ 30 Days Check Up ✓

Monthly Progress Tracker:

MONTH 5

Beginning of the first Month:		End of the first Month:	
How do I feel physically? (In a scale 1 - 5, with 5 being the best)	☐☐☐☐☐	**How do I feel physically now?** (In a scale 1 - 5, with 5 being the best)	☐☐☐☐☐
How do I feel emotionally? (In a scale 1 - 5, with 5 being the best)	☐☐☐☐☐	**How do I feel emotionally now?** (In a scale 1 - 5, with 5 being the best)	☐☐☐☐☐
How is the quality of my sleep? (In a scale 1 - 5, with 5 being the best)	☐☐☐☐☐	**How is the quality of my sleep now?** (In a scale 1 - 5, with 5 being the best)	☐☐☐☐☐
Overall Mood/wellbeing: (In a scale 1 - 5, with 5 being the best)	☐☐☐☐☐	**Overall mood/wellbeing now:** (In a scale 1 - 5, with 5 being the best)	☐☐☐☐☐

How helpful these sessions were? Which were the most important sessions of the month? Why was that?

How do I evaluate my interaction with my therapist? Do I feel heard and embraced? What are the most valuable tools he/she has given me this month to work with?

Did I notice any changes or shifts during this month? If yes, what may have contributed to the changes? What do I notice feeling now?

Important takeaways and reminders for the next month sessions (from me & from my therapist):

Meaningful Quotes & Thoughts

*"Being kind to yourself is one of the greatest kindnesses"
Remember to prioritize your mental health and people who make you feel positive and energized.*

MONTH 6

Date: **Session: #**

Next Session:

Mood Tracker

Before the Session:
← Very Good   Neutral   Not great →

After the Session:
← Very Good   Neutral   Not great →

Suggestions of things to think and write about:
(The prompts below will be the same for all the sessions because they can be a simple starting point for you to write, reflect and track your progress over time. Feel free to use them or write freely about your session)

- Topic(s) I want to discuss and goal(s) for the session.
  Reflection: How do they affect my life?

- How do I feel physically and emotionally after my session today? Any shifts in my breathing, heart rate, muscle tightness? Try to describe your thoughts and feelings.

- Did I feel heard and comfortable with my therapist today? Did I feel safe to communicate my needs and goals to her/him? Is our therapeutic relationship evolving?

- Do I already see ways to help myself to get over my symptoms and reach my goals?

- How can I use the takeaways from this session to help me with my therapy process and improve my life?

- Write about possible actions, tools you learned and follow ups from the therapist.

My Notes (from before, during and/or after session).
If you need more space, please use the Additional Notes Section at the end of this journal

....

....

....

....

....

....

The main things that I want to remember from today are:

(Some ideas: Homework, key takeaways, reminders for your next session, challenges to keep in mind and wins to be celebrated!)

MONTH 6

Date:

Session: #

Next Session:

Mood Tracker

Before the Session:
Very Good — Neutral — Not great

After the Session:
Very Good — Neutral — Not great

Suggestions of things to think and write about:
(The prompts below will be the same for all the sessions because they can be a simple starting point for you to write, reflect and track your progress over time. Feel free to use them or write freely about your session)

- Topic(s) I want to discuss and goal(s) for the session.
  Reflection: How do they affect my life?

- How do I feel physically and emotionally after my session today? Any shifts in my breathing, heart rate, muscle tightness? Try to describe your thoughts and feelings.

- Did I feel heard and comfortable with my therapist today? Did I feel safe to communicate my needs and goals to her/him? Is our therapeutic relationship evolving?

- Do I already see ways to help myself to get over my symptoms and reach my goals?

- How can I use the takeaways from this session to help me with my therapy process and improve my life?

- Write about possible actions, tools you learned and follow ups from the therapist.

My Notes (from before, during and/or after session).
If you need more space, please use the Additional Notes Section at the end of this journal

....

....

....

....

....

....

The main things that I want to remember from today are:

(Some ideas: Homework, key takeaways, reminders for your next session, challenges to keep in mind and wins to be celebrated!)

MONTH 6

Date:

Session: #

Next Session:

Mood Tracker

Before the Session:
Very Good — Neutral — Not great

After the Session:
Very Good — Neutral — Not great

Suggestions of things to think and write about:
(The prompts below will be the same for all the sessions because they can be a simple starting point for you to write, reflect and track your progress over time. Feel free to use them or write freely about your session)

- **Topic(s) I want to discuss and goal(s) for the session.
  Reflection: How do they affect my life?**

- **How do I feel physically and emotionally after my session today? Any shifts in my breathing, heart rate, muscle tightness? Try to describe your thoughts and feelings.**

- **Did I feel heard and comfortable with my therapist today? Did I feel safe to communicate my needs and goals to her/him? Is our therapeutic relationship evolving?**

- **Do I already see ways to help myself to get over my symptoms and reach my goals?**

- **How can I use the takeaways from this session to help me with my therapy process and improve my life?**

- **Write about possible actions, tools you learned and follow ups from the therapist.**

My Notes (from before, during and/or after session).
If you need more space, please use the Additional Notes Section at the end of this journal

....

....

....

....

....

....

The main things that I want to remember from today are:

(Some ideas: Homework, key takeaways, reminders for your next session, challenges to keep in mind and wins to be celebrated!)

-
-
-

MONTH 6

Date:

Session: #

Next Session:

Mood Tracker

Before the Session:
Very Good — Neutral — Not great

After the Session:
Very Good — Neutral — Not great

Suggestions of things to think and write about:
(The prompts below will be the same for all the sessions because they can be a simple starting point for you to write, reflect and track your progress over time. Feel free to use them or write freely about your session)

✎ Topic(s) I want to discuss and goal(s) for the session.
Reflection: How do they affect my life?

✎ How do I feel physically and emotionally after my session today? Any shifts in my breathing, heart rate, muscle tightness? Try to describe your thoughts and feelings.

✎ Did I feel heard and comfortable with my therapist today? Did I feel safe to communicate my needs and goals to her/him? Is our therapeutic relationship evolving?

✎ Do I already see ways to help myself to get over my symptoms and reach my goals?

✎ How can I use the takeaways from this session to help me with my therapy process and improve my life?

✎ Write about possible actions, tools you learned and follow ups from the therapist.

My Notes (from before, during and/or after session).
If you need more space, please use the Additional Notes Section at the end of this journal

The main things that I want to remember from today are:

(Some ideas: Homework, key takeaways, reminders for your next session, challenges to keep in mind and wins to be celebrated!)

MONTH 6

Date:

Next Session:

Session: #

Mood Tracker

Before the Session:
Very Good — Neutral — Not great

After the Session:
Very Good — Neutral — Not great

Suggestions of things to think and write about:
(The prompts below will be the same for all the sessions because they can be a simple starting point for you to write, reflect and track your progress over time. Feel free to use them or write freely about your session)

- Topic(s) I want to discuss and goal(s) for the session.
  Reflection: How do they affect my life?

- How do I feel physically and emotionally after my session today? Any shifts in my breathing, heart rate, muscle tightness? Try to describe your thoughts and feelings.

- Did I feel heard and comfortable with my therapist today? Did I feel safe to communicate my needs and goals to her/him? Is our therapeutic relationship evolving?

- Do I already see ways to help myself to get over my symptoms and reach my goals?

- How can I use the takeaways from this session to help me with my therapy process and improve my life?

- Write about possible actions, tools you learned and follow ups from the therapist.

My Notes (from before, during and/or after session).
If you need more space, please use the Additional Notes Section at the end of this journal

....
....
....
....
....
....
....
....
....
....
....
....
....
....

The main things that I want to remember from today are:

(Some ideas: Homework, key takeaways, reminders for your next session, challenges to keep in mind and wins to be celebrated!)

-
-
-

✓ 30 Days Check Up ✓

Monthly Progress Tracker:

MONTH 6

Beginning of the first Month:	End of the first Month:
How do I feel physically? (In a scale 1 - 5, with 5 being the best) ☐☐☐☐☐	How do I feel physically now? (In a scale 1 - 5, with 5 being the best) ☐☐☐☐☐
How do I feel emotionally? (In a scale 1 - 5, with 5 being the best) ☐☐☐☐☐	How do I feel emotionally now? (In a scale 1 - 5, with 5 being the best) ☐☐☐☐☐
How is the quality of my sleep? (In a scale 1 - 5, with 5 being the best) ☐☐☐☐☐	How is the quality of my sleep now? (In a scale 1 - 5, with 5 being the best) ☐☐☐☐☐
Overall Mood/wellbeing: (In a scale 1 - 5, with 5 being the best) ☐☐☐☐☐	Overall mood/wellbeing now: (In a scale 1 - 5, with 5 being the best) ☐☐☐☐☐

How helpful these sessions were? Which were the most important sessions of the month? Why was that?

How do I evaluate my interaction with my therapist? Do I feel heard and embraced? What are the most valuable tools he/she has given me this month to work with?

Did I notice any changes or shifts during this month? If yes, what may have contributed to the changes? What do I notice feeling now?

Important takeaways and reminders for the next month sessions (from me & from my therapist):

Meaningful Quotes & Thoughts

Remember your connection to the work you are doing in therapy!
Your journey matters, you are doing a great job,
your are becoming the best version of yourself.

Additional Notes Pages

Thank you For Using This Journal. We Hope you liked it!

We are on a journey of publishing 52 journals this year!
We would love to invite you to check out one of our other Journals:

E English **F** French **G** German **I** Italian

Therapy Journals

THERAPY JOURNAL:
E F G I

This is a journal with prompts (questions and suggestions), and it was designed to support you during 30 therapy sessions, no matter how often they take place (ie. it will be ok if you use it twice a week, once a week, or once every 2 weeks). It also includes important recommendations that will help you make the most of your therapy sessions.

ONLINE THERAPY JOURNAL:
E F G I

Similar to the above, this is a journal with prompts (questions and suggestions), and it was designed to support you during 30 virtual / telephonic therapy sessions, no matter how often they take place (eg. twice a week, once a week, or once every 2 weeks).
The difference it that this journal gives recommendations for VIRTUAL sessions.

THERAPY SESSIONS JOURNAL:
E F G I

If you like to write in LINED journals, this is the one for you! This journal also has prompts (questions & suggestions), and it was designed to support you during 6 months of therapy (with weekly therapy sessions, ie. 4-5 sessions per month). This therapy journal will help you make the most of your therapy and self-reflection sessions.!

COUPLES THERAPY JOURNAL:
E F I

This journal has 3 main spaces for you to write in: (1) a space for you to write what is the focus of each session, (2) a space to capture how your partner is thinking and feeling and what he/she is sharing, (3) and finally a space for you to write your own insights & takeaways during counseling sessions. The right choice for people attending Couples Therapy!

Therapist Journal

A THERAPIST JOURNAL:
E F I

Encouraged and guided by a professional therapist, we created this journal to provide the best help for therapists, both in their preparation for the therapy sessions, and during the sessions themselves.
This journal is what we were told would be the most efficient way for organizing therapist notes, all in one place!

Inner Peace, Resilience & Relationships

HAPPINESS FROM THE SOUL
F I

This "self-therapy" happiness journal is exactly what you need to start to implement daily 3 things that a Harvard professor teaches : Organize your errands / Message someone important/ Write a journal entry. After a few days doing this, you're very likely to start feeling happier!

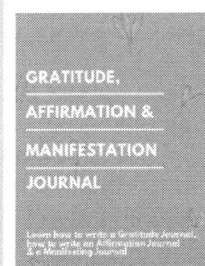

GRATITUDE, AFFIRMATION AND MANIFESTATION JOURNAL
E F G I

This journal brings it all to you: Gratitude, Affirmation & Manifestation. They together can emanates the best feelings within us and help us become calmer, more resilient and in turn help us live a happier life and give us the encouragement to pursue our goals.
This journal will help you relax and connect with the best within you to create the life of your dreams.

Kids

LET'S GO READING JOURNAL FOR CHILDREN:
E F I

This journal was created to encourage kids to have reading & discussion time with their grown ups. It also includes key recommendations for the grown ups on how to make the most of reading time with kids. And the "big readers" will have a wonderful record of the child's assisted reading journey.

SUMMER READING JOURNAL FOR CHILDREN:
E F

This child-friendly journal will help caregivers and children establish a reading routine during this summer. After going through the challenge of 25 books this summer, kids will learn to look forward to reading & discussion time, and the "big readers" will have a record of the child's reading progress made over time! This journal also includes a list of suggested activities for the summer

KIDS ACTIVITIES JOURNAL FOR CHILDREN:
E

This journal was designed to support families in developing a healthier, more organized & efficient routine of activities while raising their children. It will help you plan for playful activities, games & hobbies with children, in addition to encouraging them to do school work and help with chores.

Motherhood, Fatherhood & Family

MOMMY & ME A KEEPSAKE JOURNAL
(E)

This is a journal with prompts that will guide a mother to write about her memories and prepare her children to thrive in life by learning mom's important advice & lessons.
Fill any page, at any time, until you complete the journal, or feel that "it's ready". Then give it (back) as a treasured gift to your child!

GODMOTHER, YOUR STORY IS A GIFT JOURNAL
(E)

A godmother's gift & godchild's gift!
This journal with prompts will guide a godmother to write about her treasured memories and important recommendations that she would like to share with her godchild.
Fill any page, at any time, until you feel that "it's ready" to be gifted to your godchildren.

GRANDMA, YOUR STORY IS A GIFT JOURNAL
(E)

The best gift for grandma!
This journal will prompt a grandmother to write about her memories, special moments with the grandkid, and precious advice. Grandmas will love to share their story, and when "ready" this journal will be a treasured gift to future generations!

AUNTIE LOVES YOU FOREVER JOURNAL
(E)

This is a journal with prompts that will guide an auntie to write about her memories and prepare her nephews & nieces to thrive in life by learning important advice and lessons. Fill any page, at any time, until you complete the journal, or feel that "it's ready". Then give this precious gift (back) to your nephews & nieces!

THINGS I LOVE (AND NOT SO MUCH) ABOUT BEING A MOM:
(E) (F) (I)

This is a blank / lined journal for moms to write about motherhood experiences – good and bad days – and make the most out of all of their days. It will help you normalize what's normal, feel more relaxed and clear your mind. And over time you will have a beautiful collection of "motherhood moments"!

FATHER YOUR STORY IS A GIFT JOURNAL
(E)

This is a journal with prompts that will guide a father to write about his memories and prepare his children to thrive in life by learning dad's important advice & lessons.
Fill any page, at any time, until you complete the journal, or feel that "it's ready". Then give it (back) as a treasured gift to your child!

PRIDE FATHER, YOUR STORY IS A GIFT JOURNAL

This is a journal with prompts that will guide a father to write about his memories and prepare his children to thrive in life by learning dad's important advice & lessons.
Fill any page, at any time, until you complete the journal, or feel that "it's ready". Then give it (back) as a treasured gift to your child!

GRANDFATHER JOURNAL. A GRANDPARENT MEMORY BOOK
(E)

The best gift for grandpa!
This journal will prompt a grandfather to write about her memories, special moments with the grandkid, and precious advice. Grandpas will love to share their story, and when "ready" this journal will be a treasured gift to future generations!

... and more!

Check our full collection on Amazon.

★ ★ ★ ★ ★

Journals available in other Languages

Our journals are available on Amazon in English, German, French, and Italian
(with more languages to come soon).

Join our "Launch Team"

If you would like to to receive free samples of future journals to help us validate concepts, with cover visual selection and more, please let us know!

--> New journals are launched almost every week! <--

Connect with us & Leave your Review on Amazon

If for any reason you are not satisfied with your journal,
please contact us directly;
we will do our best to make you happy!

And, especially if you're happy with the journal,
we'd really appreciate if you could leave an honest review on Amazon
(even just the star rating helps us a lot!)

We would love to stay connected, and receive your comments or suggestions.
Follow / message / tag us / leave a review:
- on Amazon: A Day to Remember Journals
- Instagram: @adaytoremember_journals
- OR email: adaytoremember.journals@gmail.com.

With much gratitude,
Carla and Milena

Made in the USA
Las Vegas, NV
05 December 2023